C Is For Colorado

By Gayle Corbett Shirley
Illustrated by Constance Rummel Bergum

ABC
PRESS

Helena, Montana

For Jesse — G.C.S.

For my family
and in memory of Larry Hayes
— C.R.B.

Copyright © 1989 by ABC Press, Helena, Montana.

Library of Congress Number: 89-83793
ISBN 0-937959-81-2 softcover
ISBN 0-937959-85-5 hardcover

Published by ABC Press, 842 Sixth Avenue, Helena, Montana 59601. Typesetting and other prepress work done at Falcon Press Publishing Co., Inc., Helena, Montana. Printed in Singapore.

Edited by Sally K. Hilander

Acknowledgments: The author and illustrator would like to thank the following people for sharing their expert knowledge of Colorado: Sally Hilander; Marshall and Jean Corbett; Bob Tully, Cher Threlkeld, and Jim Bennett, with the Colorado Division of Wildlife; and Deborah Milo, public relations director of the Colorado Office of Tourism. Also, thanks to the National Football League, for permission to use the Denver Bronco emblem.

To order additional copies

To order additional copies of *C is for Colorado,* please send $12.95 (hardcover) or $6.95 (softcover), plus $1.50 each for postage and handling to: ABC Press, 842 Sixth Avenue, Helena, Montana, 59601. Be sure to specify the number of copies you want, and include your name and complete address, including zip code, with your order. Please allow three to four weeks for delivery.

For information about bulk orders and retailer discounts, call ABC Press at (406) 442-4992, or write the above address.

On the cover: Pikes Peak; Rocky Mountain bighorn sheep, the state animal; lark bunting, the state bird; columbine, the state flower.

A is for aspen

Aspens quaking in the wind
Are quite a sight to see.
The golden leaves whisper my name
And seem to wink at me.

B is for bison

Once the beat of bison hooves
Was loud upon the plains.
Then greedy hunters killed the beasts.
Now only an echo remains.

C is for cowboy

When a cowboy climbs aboard a bronc
He knows to hold on tight.
For the bucking brute will do its best
To launch him into flight.

D is for Denver

The city of Denver is called "Mile High,"
But it's not floating in the sky.
Nor do its buildings stand that tall.
It's a mile above the sea, that's all.

 **is for elk**

A mighty crown of antlers
And a bugle shrill and clear
Can help you tell the regal elk
From other kinds of deer.

F is for fossil

The fearsome dinosaurs are gone,
And all they've left behind
Are chunks of bone now turned to stone—
A thrilling fossil find.

G is for ghost town

A ghost town has no spooks who scare.
It's just a reminder of folks once there
Who searched for gold amid the dust,
Then left when the mining boom went bust.

 **H is for hiker**

A ribbon of trail unwinding
Before a hiker's feet
May lead her to a special place—
A wild, unspoiled retreat.

I is for Indian

Some Indians of long ago,
While worrying about their foes,
Decided they'd be safer if
They built their homes into a cliff.

 **J is for jet**

Thunder rumbling in the sky
Could mean a jet is streaking by.
When I dash outside to see,
The lightning trail convinces me.

K is for kayaker

Taming a wild river
With a paddle and a prayer,
The kayaker finds thrills and spills
Where others wouldn't dare.

L is for lake

A lake is like a looking glass,
But through the mirror lies
A world swimming with creatures
Of exotic shape and size.

M is for mountains

Mountains raw and jagged
Stretch their peaks up high.
If we choose to climb them,
They're our ladders to the sky.

N is for nugget

The thought of wealth lured people west.
"Pike's Peak or bust!" they vowed.
Gold nuggets were the magnets
That attracted such a crowd.

O is for oil

Sometimes oil is called "black gold."
It pools deep underground.
You can tell its presence
By the derricks all around.

P is for pika

While climbing high atop Pikes Peak,
You may be startled by a squeak
That seems to come from underground.
The tiny pika makes that sound.

Q is for quilt

When frigid weather comes to stay,
You can keep the cold at bay.
Tuck a quilt all snug and tight
Around you as you sleep at night.

R is for rattlesnake

The rattlesnake sounds vicious
With its rattle, hiss, and spit.
But it's just as afraid of me
As I am scared of it.

S is for skier

Two long slats strapped to her feet,
Two poles held in her hands,
The skier plows a zig-zag course
Through a snowy wonderland.

T is for train

All aboard the train that runs
From Durango to Silverton!
Take a wild, historic ride
On tracks that hug a mountainside.

U is for up

I'd love to float with a giant balloon
Up into the air so high
That I could reach out and pull a wisp
From a cottony cloud drifting by.

 **is for vista**

Vista means a distant view,
And in this state you'll find
Scenery that's spectacular
And views of every kind.

W is for wheat

Green wheat reaching for the sun
Turns to gold when summer's done.
Combines take the grain's ripe head.
Bakers bake it into bread.

X is at Four Corners

There's only one place where four states meet
Creating an X you can see at your feet—
Where Arizona, Utah, and New Mexico
All touch a corner of Colorado.

 **Y** is for yucca

Indians used the yucca
To make sandals, cloth, and rope.
They cooked and ate the seed pods,
And the roots they turned to soap.

 **is for zoo**

When I'm visiting the zoo,
I often wonder why
The needle-necked giraffe and I
Cannot see eye to eye.

Learn more about it

As you were reading this book, you may have noticed that each picture contained several things common to Colorado that began with the accompanying letter. You may want to go back and read the book again and see how many of them you can name. The following guide will help you. It also will tell you more about each of the things that are pictured.

Aspen: The quaking aspen is one of the most common trees in the Colorado mountains. It has oval, pointed, fine-toothed leaves. The stems of the leaves are flat, which causes the leaves to tremble in the smallest breeze. The leaves turn gold and sometimes red in the fall. One excellent place to see the bright fall foliage of the aspen is in Phantom Canyon, which runs north from Florence to Cripple Creek in Pikes Peak Country.

Antelope: Although commonly called an antelope, this deer-like animal is more accurately known as a pronghorn. It's the fastest animal in North America. It can run as fast as 60 miles an hour—about as fast as your car goes on an interstate highway. The antelope prefers to live on the rolling prairies of eastern Colorado.

Avocet: The avocet is a shorebird. It lives near lakes, rivers, and marshes. It wades in shallow water with its long legs. It uses its thin, upcurved bill to feed on insects and shellfish that swim near the surface of the water.

Bison (also called buffalo): When explorer Stephen Long visited Colorado in 1819, a member of his party reported seeing many bison grazing on the plains. But by the late 1800s, bison had almost disappeared. Hunters had been shooting them by the thousands because people wanted to make robes from their hides. The last four wild bison in Colorado were killed in 1897. Today, you can see bison at two parks near Denver—Daniel's Park southwest of the city and Genesee Park to the west. While at Genesee, you can also visit the nearby grave of famous buffalo hunter William F. Cody, who was better known as Buffalo Bill.

Beargrass: The long, thin leaves of beargrass grow in bunches on mountain slopes and in alpine meadows. The plant looks very much like grass, except it has a tall stalk with small white flowers clustered at the top. Bears do like to eat parts of the plant. So do elk and mountain goats.

Brown bat: This is one of the most common kinds of bat in the nation. It's not afraid of people, and it lives in occupied or empty buildings as well as in caves. It likes to eat insects.

Cowboy: You can learn more about rodeo cowboys at the Prorodeo Hall of Champions and Museum of the American Cowboy in Colorado Springs. If you're lucky, there may be a rodeo going on while you're in town. Rodeos are held during the summer in many Colorado communities. You can also learn more about what a cowboy does by attending the National Western Stock Show. It's held every January in Denver. It's the world's largest livestock show.

Cactus: Cacti are made to withstand the hot, dry climate of the desert. They can store water in their leaves. In an emergency, you could drink some of this water by cutting into the cactus' stem, but it would taste bitter. The fruit of the cactus tastes better, either raw or cooked. Be sure to peel away the prickly skin before you take a bite!

Coyote: Along with the pronghorn antelope and the prairie dog, the coyote is one of the most common animals in eastern Colorado. Farmers and ranchers often don't like it because it kills and eats chickens and young cows and sheep. But the coyote also can be helpful to farmers and ranchers. It eats insects and small rodents that damage grain fields and pastures.

Denver: Denver is the capital of Colorado and the largest city in the Rocky Mountain West. It's situated at 5,280 feet—one mile—above sea level. That's why it's nicknamed the "Mile-High City." Denver sprang up in 1858 when a group of prospectors set up camp there. The city was named after James Denver, who was governor of Kansas Territory at the time. The city is home to a branch of the U.S. Mint, which makes more than 5 million coins a year, and the Denver Broncos, a professional football team whose emblem is pictured. You can also visit the Capitol Building. It has a dome covered with gold that was mined in Colorado.

Elk: The elk is the largest kind of deer except for the moose. It's sometimes called by its Indian name, *wapiti*. By the beginning of this century, the number of elk in Colorado had dwindled, possibly because they were being hunted so heavily. Then some elk were brought here from other states. Today, more than 175,000 elk can be found living in various parts of Colorado. One particularly good place to see them is in Rocky Mountain National Park, where about 3,000 of them live.

Eagle: Both bald and golden eagles nest in Colorado. The bald eagle—symbol of our nation—is an endangered species. That means it's in danger of disappearing altogether if a special effort isn't made to help it survive by protecting the places in which it lives. You can see bald eagles during the winter at Jackson Lake State Recreation Area, 80 miles northeast of Denver, and at Boulder Mountain Park on the western edge of Boulder. You can also see them during winter at Bonny State Recreation Area, near the Colorado-Kansas border. Bonny is considered one of the best places in Colorado for birdwatching. In winter, as many as 50,000 birds live there, and more than 70,000 fly over during spring and fall.

Fossil: Many kinds of fossils have been found in Colorado. At Dinosaur National Monument on the Colorado-Utah border, you can see the 140-million-year-old bones of 10 kinds of dinosaur, including the stegosaurus and the fierce allosaurus shown in the picture. The stegosaurus is the state fossil. Florissant Fossil Beds National Monument, 35 miles west of Colorado Springs, is famous for its petrified trees and its plant and insect fossils.

Fairyslipper: You're likely to spot this dainty flower growing on or near rotting stumps and logs in mountain forests. It likes shade and wet earth.

Ghost town: When gold and silver were discovered in Colorado, many people rushed west, hoping to get rich. They quickly built towns in which to live while they searched for their fortunes. They created what is known as a mining "boom." When no more gold or silver could be found, the miners moved on. The empty towns they left behind became ghost towns, evidence of a mining "bust." Today you can visit some of these ghost towns. They have colorful names like Silver Plume, Kokomo, Marble, Saint Elmo, Alta, and Animas Forks. Some have been restored to give visitors a better idea of what life was like during the boom years. These include Central City, Black Hawk, Georgetown, Crested Butte, Silverton, and Cripple Creek, the richest goldfield in Colorado.

Grebe: Like the duck, the grebe is an expert swimmer. It lives near ponds and lakes. It eats fish and other creatures that it catches by diving underwater. The grebe is very clumsy on land. Its legs are so far back on its body that it can't walk upright.

Geranium: The wild geranium can be found along roads and creeks and in woods and meadows. Moose, elk, and deer love its taste. Even bears will make a meal of it.

Hiker: Colorado is a wonderful place to hike because it has so many kinds of landscape. You can climb a mountain, walk along the rim of a canyon, slog through sand dunes, or hunt for wildflowers in a prairie meadow. You can hike the Colorado Trail, which stretches from Denver to Durango. It's a special feeling to hike through the wilderness, imagining you're the first person who's ever been there. Be sure to leave the land as you found it, so that others can have this experience, too.

Heron: The great blue heron (pictured) is an excellent fisherman. It stands perfectly still in shallow water, waiting for fish to swim near. Then it lunges forward, grabbing small fish or spearing large ones with its sharp beak. It also likes to eat frogs, lizards, snakes, insects, mice, and squirrels.

Horse: More than 550 wild horses graze the grasses of Colorado. They make up four herds, all of which live in the western part of the state near the Utah border. Wild horses usually are the descendants of Indian ponies or horses that have escaped from their owners. For the past 15 years, the U.S. government has allowed people to "adopt" some of these wild horses and tame them.

Indian: The Arapahoes, Cheyennes, Kiowas, Navajos, Utes, and ancient Anasazi all have made Colorado their home. The most awesome remains of the Anasazi civilization can be seen at Mesa Verde National Park in southwestern Colorado. There, Indian villages built between 700 and 1,500 years ago are nestled in sandstone cliffs. You can see more Anasazi ruins at nearby Hovenweep National Monument, Yucca House National Monument, Mountain Tribal Park, and Lowry Pueblo Ruins. The only Indian reservations in Colorado belong to the Southern and Mountain Utes. They're in the southwestern corner of the state. If you visit in summer, you can watch Indians in colorful costumes perform ceremonial dances.

Ilia underwing moth: This common type of moth spends its days resting on tree trunks, where the coloring of its upper wings makes it hard to see. It hides its colorful underwings while at rest. The moth is most active at night. It's attracted to light, so you may see it swarming around porch lights or near lit up doors or windows.

Iris: Indians once used the roots of the wild iris to make a poison in which they dipped their arrows. When someone was wounded with one of these arrows, even only slightly, he supposedly would die within a week. Obviously, you should not eat this plant.

Jet: Military jets often can be heard streaking through the sky above Colorado. That's because Colorado Springs is home to the U.S. Air Force Academy and Peterson Air Force Base. The U.S. Space Command Center, the North American Defense Command, and Fort Carson Army Base are also located there.

Jackrabbit: You can tell the jackrabbit from a cottontail by its very long ears and hind legs. The jackrabbit's long ears not only help it hear well, they also help it stay cool. When blood flows through the veins in the ears, it's cooled by the air as the rabbit hops about. Some jackrabbits turn white in winter, so that they can hide better in the snow.

Jacobs-ladder: If you climb high into the mountains, you may spot the dainty Jacobs-ladder peeking from rock crevices. Don't step on one! When crushed, the flower has a horrible smell that can haunt you all day.

Kayaker: About 200,000 people paddle kayaks or row rafts on Colorado rivers each year. The most popular rivers are the Arkansas, which runs through Royal Gorge near Canon City, and the Colorado, which begins in Rocky Mountain National Park and empties into the Gulf of California in Mexico.

Kangaroo rat: This desert animal got its name because it leaps like a kangaroo when it runs. It lives underground and comes out mostly at night.

Kestrel: This bird of prey is also called a sparrow hawk. It hovers in the air or perches on telephone wires, poles, or dead branches, watching for the small birds and animals it likes to eat.

Lake: Colorado is not known for its natural lakes. Most lakes in the state were formed when rivers were dammed. Blue Mesa Lake west of Gunnison is Colorado's largest man-made lake. It's 20 miles long and has 96 miles of shoreline. Grand Lake on the western edge of Rocky Mountain National Park is the largest natural lake.

Ladybird beetle: Often called ladybug, this common insect is usually red-orange with black spots. It can be a good bug to have around, because it eats other insects such as aphids and mites, which are harmful to gardens and orchards.

Leopard frog: A good jumper and swimmer, the leopard frog likes to live in cattail marshes and shallow streams. It can croak both on or under water.

Lupine: The lupine got its name from *lupus,* the Latin word for wolf, because people once mistakenly thought that the wildflower robbed the soil of important minerals. The lupine is related to peas and green beans, but you shouldn't try to eat one. The seeds are poisonous.

Mountains (the San Juans are shown): Of the 67 peaks in the United States that are higher than 14,000 feet, 54 are in Colorado. Mount Elbert, at 14,433 feet, is the highest mountain in the state and the second highest in the nation. Only Mount Whitney in California is higher. The most famous mountain in Colorado is Pikes Peak. When Katherine Lee Bates rode to its top in 1895, the view inspired her to write the words to "America, the Beautiful."

Mountain lion: The mountain lion is also called a cougar or puma. It's the largest cat in America. It eats deer, elk, and rabbits and other small animals. In Colorado, it can be found anywhere there are lots of deer or elk. It's very strong and can leap 40 feet. Mountain lions are secretive creatures. Few people ever see one.

Moose: The moose is the largest member of the deer family. Colorado State Forest State Park in north-central Colorado is one of the best places in the state to see moose. You may see them wandering through the willow thickets along the Michigan River.

Nugget: Gold fever hit Colorado in 1858 when a miner found some nuggets in a creek near present-day Denver. When even more gold was discovered the following year, about 100,000 fortune-seekers set out for Colorado. Some of them painted the words "Pike's Peak or Bust" on the sides of their covered wagons. About half never made it to the gold fields. Of those who did, many didn't find the fortunes they were looking for.

Night heron: As you might guess from its name, this long-legged wading bird is active at night. During the day it roosts in bushes and trees.

Oil: You may spot oil derricks while driving through northern Colorado.

They form towers over the sites where people are drilling for oil. The second oil well in the United States was discovered on Oil Creek near Florence in 1862.

Owl: The barn owl (pictured) is said to be monkey-faced. Can you see why? It hunts at night for mice, rabbits, and birds. During the day, it hides out in barns, hollow trees, church towers, and deserted buildings. The barn owl can turn its head all the way around and look backwards.

Onion: Indians added flavor to their meals by using the wild onion. So did the famous explorers Lewis and Clark. Black bears and squirrels like the bulbs, but elk and deer prefer the leaves.

Pika: The tiny pika may look like a mouse but it's a member of the rabbit family. It lives under rocks high in the mountains. Even though it's very small, it makes a loud chirping sound when alarmed.

Pikes Peak: Pikes Peak was named after Zebulon Pike, who explored the Colorado area in 1806. Pike was unable to climb the mountain. In fact, he thought no one ever could. He was wrong. Today, hundreds of thousands of people go to the top by foot, car, or cog railway.

Pasqueflower: This beautiful flower begins blooming in March, an early sign of spring. It contains an oil that has been used in medicine.

Quilt: Crusading knights discovered quilts in the Middle East almost a thousand years ago. Their womenfolk adopted the idea and began quilting clothing and bed coverings to keep their families warm during cold winters in chilly castles.

Quail: The Gambel's quail (pictured) can usually be found near water in brushy desert areas of southwestern Colorado.

Rattlesnake: Watch out for this poisonous reptile. It lives in all kinds of places, from brushy lowlands to high mountain slopes, from prairies to forests. If you disturb it, it will try to warn you away with a loud buzzing noise it makes by shaking the rattle on the end of its tail. Given the chance, it will flee rather than bite you. Rattlers can be helpful, too. They eat some kinds of pests, such as insects and small mice.

Ringtail cat: It's easy to recognize this relative of the raccoon. It has a long tail with white and blackish-brownish rings. It prefers to live in dry, rough country. You may not be able to spot one, though. It comes out mostly at night.

Rose: Like the garden rose, the wild rose protects itself with thorns. But if you're careful, you can pick its fruit, called rose hips. They can be eaten raw or made into jelly. Indians and early settlers used them for food. Bears, pheasants, grouse, and quail like to eat them, too.

Skier: Colorado is famous for its skiing. Seven of the state's 27 ski areas are considered among the 10 best in the country. Vail, 100 miles west of Denver, is the largest and most popular ski resort in the nation. Cross-country skiing is also popular. Many ski resorts have cross-country trails. Or you can just set out across a meadow or mountainside on your own.

Shooting star: This flower was named for its flaring shape. It often blooms early, in late April or early May. Elk and deer eat it then, when other green plants are still scarce.

Skunk: If you don't recognize this unwelcome creature by its black and white fur, you'll definitely know it by its smell. When it's frightened, the skunk squirts a very stinky substance from a gland beneath its tail. That's enough to send most predators running.

Squirrel: The Abert's squirrel (pictured) is sometimes called a tassle-eared squirrel. It's easy to see why. Unlike other squirrels, it doesn't store food for the winter. Instead, it feeds on the inner bark of branches. In summer, it prefers pine cones.

Train: The Durango-to-Silverton narrow gauge railroad was built in 1881. It hauled gold, silver, and other ore from the San Juan Mountains. Today it carries tourists. The train runs 45 miles through a remote wilderness canyon, alongside the Animas River. You can climb aboard at Durango, in southwestern Colorado. You can also ride the narrow-gauge rails of the Cumbres & Toltec Scenic Railroad, which originates in Antonito and travels through the San Juan Mountains. Or you can explore mines and ghost towns while riding the Cripple Creek-Victor Narrow Gauge, which has one of the few steam locomotives left in the country. In historic Georgetown, where silver was mined, you can board the Georgetown Loop Railroad.

Thistle: You'll usually find this spiny weed in mountain meadows. Indians used the fleshy roots and stems for food. An early explorer of Yellowstone National Park, after becoming lost, survived for a month by eating almost nothing but thistle roots. The peeled stems are tender and have a sweet, delicate taste. Thistles are a favorite food of elk and bears.

Turkey: Benjamin Franklin, the famous statesman and scientist, thought the turkey, not the bald eagle, should be our national bird. The eagle has a "bad moral character," he said, because it steals food from other birds. Turkeys are "more respectable" and are "true, original natives of America," he thought. Maybe it's best that Franklin didn't get his way. The turkey is pretty ugly, with its caruncles, wattle, and snood. Caruncles are the bumps on the turkey's neck and head. They change color from red to blue to white, depending upon the bird's mood. The wattle is the fleshy growth on the turkey's throat, while the snood extends from its forehead.

Up: Balloonists seem to like Colorado. About 250 giant, brightly colored balloons drift up into the sky above the Denver area every August, when the RE/MAX Balloon Invitational is held. There are also balloon festivals in Aspen, Avon, Carbondale, Colorado Springs, Fort Collins, Grand Junction, Loveland, Montrose, and Rocky Ford.

Ursa Major: On a clear night, you can see this constellation above you. It includes the stars that form the Big Dipper.

Vista: Through the window in the picture, you can see Great Sand Dunes National Monument, where the dunes are higher than anywhere else in the country; the Garden of the Gods, where sandstone rocks form strange and awesome shapes; and the Collegiate Peaks of the Sawatch Mountain Range, where, as the name suggests, the peaks were named for colleges.

Violet-green swallow: This sparrow-sized bird can be found in many kinds of places—meadows, ranches, plains, foothills, mountains, canyons, and cliffs. It spends much of its time flying after the insects it likes to eat.

Wheat: Colorado farmers make more money selling winter wheat than any other crop. Large fields of it can be seen waving in the wind in the eastern part of the state.

Weasel: Although weasels are common in Colorado, they're seldom seen. This is probably because they're most active at night. Like a cat, the weasel can hiss, scream, and purr. It's very ferocious for its size.

Wood lily: This beautiful flower is in danger of disappearing because people often pick it before it has a chance to drop its seeds. Wildflowers are lovely, but they wilt soon after they're picked. When you spot a pretty flower, leave it for the next person to enjoy, too.

X (Four Corners): The borders of Colorado, Utah, Arizona, and New Mexico all meet at Four Corners Monument. A large cement pad, built in 1961, marks the site. This is the only place in the country where you can stand in four states at the same time.

X (marks the spot): When ranchers want to mark their cattle so that everyone knows who owns them, they use brands like those shown around the map. The brands are burned into the animals' hides with a hot branding iron. At last count, Colorado had more than 33,000 registered brands.

Yucca: The yucca plant grows in dry, sandy soil. It has stiff, sword-shaped leaves. The leaves have fibers that can be separated out and used to make rope, sandals, and cloth. The roots get sudsy in water, so the Indians and early settlers used them to wash their clothes and hair. Indians also ate the green seed pods after baking them in ashes or drying them in the sun. You probably wouldn't want to do so, because they taste bitter.

Yellow-headed blackbird: This easily recognized bird lives in fields, marshes, and farmyards. It eats seeds and bugs.

Zoo: The Cheyenne Mountain Zoo in Colorado Springs specializes in raising giraffes. It's the major supplier of giraffes to zoos all over the country. You can see more than 150 other kinds of wild animals there, too. The Denver Zoo holds about 300 kinds of animals.

It has a large collection of North American wildlife, including hooved animals such as the antelope and bison. You can also see many kinds of birds there. The Pueblo Zoo features about 70 kinds of animals, including many cold-blooded amphibians and reptiles. It also has a "discovery room," where you can look through microscopes or make "critter tracks."

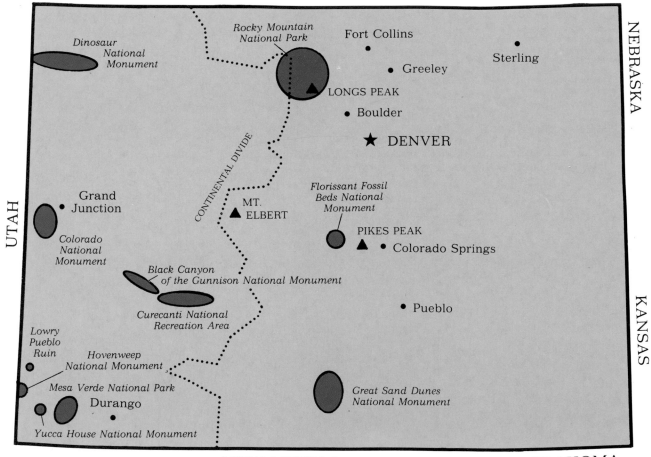

WYOMING

NEBRASKA

Dinosaur National Monument

Rocky Mountain National Park

Fort Collins

Sterling

Greeley

▲ LONGS PEAK

Boulder

★ DENVER

UTAH

CONTINENTAL DIVIDE

Grand Junction

MT. ▲ ELBERT

Florissant Fossil Beds National Monument

Colorado National Monument

PIKES PEAK

▲ Colorado Springs

Black Canyon of the Gunnison National Monument

Curecanti National Recreation Area

Pueblo

Lowry Pueblo Ruin

Hovenweep National Monument

Mesa Verde National Park

Durango

Great Sand Dunes National Monument

KANSAS

Yucca House National Monument

NEW MEXICO

OKLAHOMA